INTRODUCTION

Visuals are becoming more and more prominent today. In 2014, the Open University published a Report on Innovation Pedagogy (M. SHARPLES and al. 2014)

- A reflexive journal (a document to record the progress of your learning)
- Mind mapping

Indeed, mind mapping and visual learning enable to:

- ☑ connect ideas
- ☑ get the big picture and zoom on details
- ☑ memorize
- ☑ present information
- ☑ take notes

Taking notes is at the heart of a student's job. Indeed, as a student, you start taking notes from the very beginning of your course. You also take notes about written sources when reading texts, making summaries, doing research work.

Taking notes is a complex process which happens in a fraction of a second. You first perceive the sound, the voice of the teacher. You should consider: Can I hear well in this part of the class? Is there any background noise? Some chatting? Is your smartphone or Facebook on your computer catching all your attention? As a second step, you need to make sense of what you hear, or in other words, switch on the understanding process (which does not always happen right on the spot). Only then will you decide on what to write down. Finally, you will proceed with note-taking.

However, by fear of missing something, some students often take extensive notes, writing down each single word they hear. Maybe some abbreviations or other techniques are used to save time. Yet, quite often, notes remain indigestible. In addition, note-taking usually happens in a linear way. Line after line, page after page. In the end, it is difficult to keep a global view and to link items together.

An excellent tool to remedy this is tree-like note-taking or mind mapping. As you only write key-words, it will help you deal with the speed of speech. Indeed, we speak a lot faster than we write. In addition, by taking notes with a mind map, you work on the big picture and the detailed view at the same time, which helps better understanding and memorizing. So ready for a more effective and successful learning?

Table of contents

CHAPTER 1:

DISCOVER MIND MAPPING

Mind mapping was developed in the 1970s by an English psychologist named Tony Buzan. The pattern of a mind map has its roots in similar forms derived from medieval thinking. The temperance map, for instance, dating from the 16th century, displayed words around a center (Delengaigne, 2016).

1.1 Study with mind mapping

Tony Buzan started developing mind mapping when he was a student. An anecdote in his biography (Keene, 2013) tells how he wanted to learn more about his brain in order to better use it for optimal learning results. He went to the library and asked for a book on this subject. The documentalist directed him to the anatomy section. He did not find what he really wanted: a book on how to use his brain more efficiently. Thereafter, his battle horse became mental literacy. That is how Tony Buzan developed a tool compatible with the physiological functioning of the human brain.

In its beginnings, mind mapping was used mainly in the world of education, especially to help children struggling with school work. In the 1970s, Tony Buzan conducted an educational experiment. He helped young people with academic difficulties to successfully complete their degree through innovative teaching methods such as mind mapping. This experience was filmed by the BBC (Buzan T., 2004).

- What is the difference between a list and mind mapping?

A list represents a closed series of items or closed thoughts. It is used for classifying a sequence of finite elements, for example a shopping list. A mind map displays open thoughts and is used to explore a subject in a tree-like shape. These branches open up to further items or ideas.

1.1.1 Adopt mind mapping as a tool to study

Tony Buzan presents mind mapping as the Swiss Army knife of intelligence. As part of your studies, mind mapping will help you to:

- **Generate ideas**

Mind mapping is a tool to develop your creativity and to brainstorm. Imagine you want to give a workshop on mind mapping but do not know where to start. You can begin with a brainstorming map. At the center of your map, you indicate the topic under discussion: mind mapping training. Then, you start generating ideas and displaying them around the center.

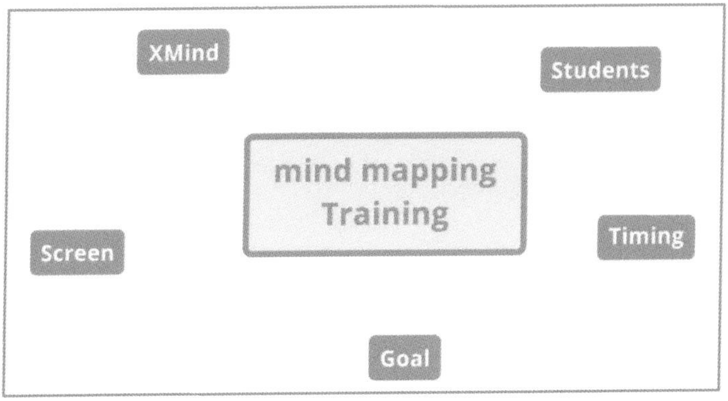

Fig: Draw a brainstorming map to generate ideas.

As you proceed, you can group your ideas into clusters. This will enable you to define categories and generate new ideas.

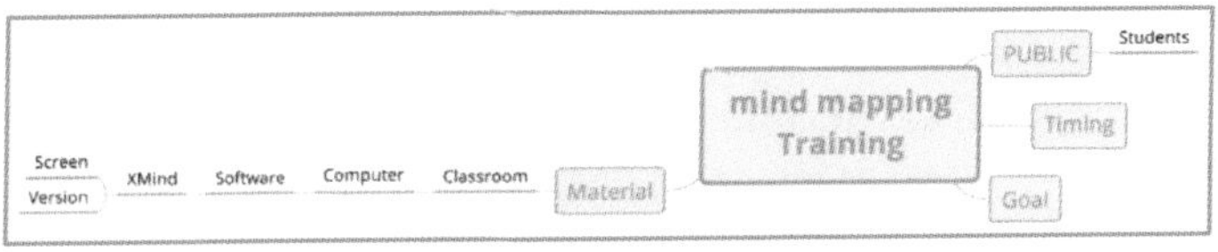

Fig: Group ideas into clusters.

To enhance creativity, you can also work the other way around, by opening unexpected paths for thought. Instead of starting at the center of the map, why not, start from the periphery and go back to the center? By changing the usual way of proceeding, new ideas will emerge. The map below expands upwards from the tip of the branch back to the center. Starting from XMind (a mind-mapping software), you think of computer, which makes you think of classroom and then of material.

Take notes

You can take notes from a written or an oral source. Taking notes while reading and analyzing a text or at a conference or while attending a lesson.

- **Write**

You can write a variety of texts or essays using mind mapping. Mind mapping will be particularly useful for writing lengthy pieces of writing such as an internship report, a dissertation or even an entire PhD thesis.

When you choose mind mapping to write a text, make sure the software you use can export in text word/text format (XMind, FreeMind).

A mind mapping software named Docear is especially designed for research. It is a software that couples the mind mapping software FreeMind with Zotero, a software to manage reference search.

- **Writer's block**

Mind mapping can help relieve those suffering from writer's block. Start by brainstorming on your topic. Organize the ideas produced at that stage and come up with a plan. Then, enrich your plan with other ideas. You should start by developing those ideas in the form of short paragraphs. Place them on sub-branches, so as to see your whole text at once. Move these paragraphs around to rearrange your text. Once your map is finalized, export it in a word processor.

- **Speak in public**

Mind mapping is also a tool which contributes to acquiring better speaking skills.

Indeed, quite often when you speak, you stay too close to your notes. In the worst case, you literally read your text. At best, you glance at your notes. With mind mapping, you will not go through this process as there are no complete sentences but only keywords to read. Moreover, the images in your map will clearly signpost the course of your presentation. The process of elaborating and building your map will contribute to better memorize and internalize your presentation.

- **Manage a project**

The benefit of mind mapping in project management is that it makes it easy to split a project into tasks and sub-tasks. It is mostly relevant at the start phase of the project. Then, for the follow-up of a project, Gantt charts are often used, as they help displaying the evolution of a task in time, and in interaction with other tasks.

1.1.2 Take the best out of mind mapping?

Mind mapping is not only a valuable tool to use throughout your studies. It is also a tool that can bring a positive contribution to your professional life. A lifelong tool, in a way.

The benefits you will gain from mind-mapping are the following:

- **Making the big picture visible**

Courses often contain plenty of details. You will probably get lost at some point. Mind-mapping will enable you to prioritize information and organize it. You will, at the same time, get the big picture (on the main branches) and have immediate access to the details (on the sub-branches).

- **Connecting ideas**

Quite often, classes are organized in a silo system, i.e. piling up information without necessarily connecting the ideas seen in economics with those seen in law, for instance. Mind mapping fosters this ability to make links. Furthermore, in a text, ideas are often presented separately. Mind mapping will allow you to connect ideas within a text. Indeed, connections are easier to make between concepts expressed by a single word, rather than a series of words or sentences.

- **Developing your creativity**

Education does not always foster the creativity of students. Yet, it is essential both for your studies as well as in a professional context.

- **Separating the wheat from the chaff**

In a text, the main ideas are drowned in many details. Mind mapping will make it possible to make these ideas stand out.

- **Giving a more personal touch and a more personal structure to your notes**

Making a mind map requires a personal way of processing information. This makes mind-maps easier to memorize by elaborating your own information architecture. For instance, the plan and the structure of a text correspond to the thoughts of the author. However, to memorize and to process information, it is needed to classify it in a more personal way, and each person structures information differently.

The illustration below shows how main ideas emerge and connect. Key ideas, keywords and key sentences are highlighted. Lines draw the link between ideas. This could be the starting point of a mind-map. This process could be applied to any text in any language.

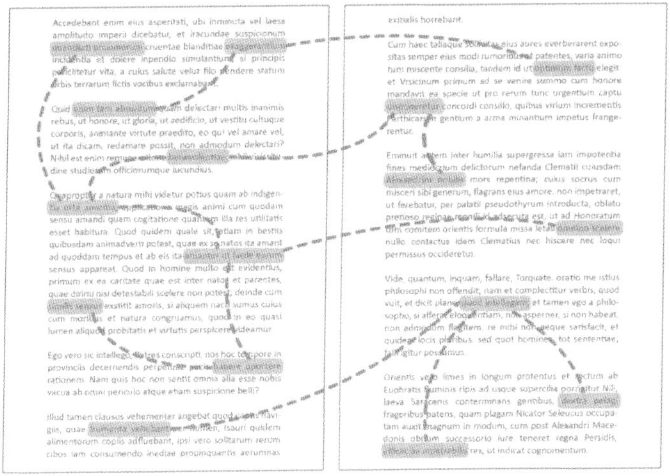

Fig: Highlight keywords and key sentences to make ideas emerge and connect.

1.1.3 Don't become a mind mapping fundamentalist!

Mind mapping embraces so many applications that you may be tempted to use it indiscriminately. However, even if mind mapping is suitable for 75% of cases, sometimes, it isn't the right tool. Define your objective first and then, choose the appropriate (visual) tool. For example, if you want to compare two concepts, the Venn diagram, which uses overlapping circles, may be more appropriate.

1.2 Build a mind-map

1.2.1 Incorporate the appropriate ingredients in your map

A mind map contains **8 ingredients**:

1) Key words

In a mind map, you don't use sentences but keywords, as it is faster to catch for the eye (and the brain). Yet, choosing the right keyword will undoubtedly be challenging. It requires practice to identify and summarize the essential elements.

2) Pictures

They are not meant to illustrate your map in order to make it pretty. They are used to express your thoughts visually. They also stimulate the right hemisphere of your brain, which is more sensitive to images and colors.

3) Pictograms

They are used to illustrate your ideas. When you take notes in relation to a text, they will help to establish an interaction between you and what the author wrote.

4) Colors

Colors highlight information and can also group elements visually. For instance, you can draw a green or yellow branch. They also stimulate memorizing.

5) The center

A mind map has one and only one center, which is the core idea and the core of your thinking process. Its central position is essential. Indeed, for human beings, vision is better at the center than at the periphery. Thus, you will stay focused on the topic and avoid going off-track.

The center is also important for students with a Dys/disorder (Dyslexics, Dyspraxics etc.). Indeed, these students suffer from a poorer short-term memory. Keeping the theme at the center will prevent forgetting too quickly.

6) Clouds

Clouds or frames make it possible to group the information visually. They are also used to create clusters and group information together.

7) Branches

Branches start from the core and spread all around it. Main branches and sub branches help to set a structure and prioritize information.

8) Links

A line or arrow can help connecting ideas located at different places on the map.

1.2.2 Follow this simple recipe

Let's practice and create a mind-map by following this simple recipe:

1. **Start in the center**: write down the theme of the map. Add an image.
2. **Generate ideas**: launch a brainstorming. Do not censor the ideas that pop into your head. Write them down.
3. **Reorganize your map**: move some branches, delete others.
   If you made a hand-drawn map, it will be more difficult to move branches around or delete them
4. **Let it rest** and review your map later.

To follow this recipe, you will be faced with a choice: should I opt for pen and paper or for a mapping software? There is no bad choice, it simply has to match your needs and intentions. To help you choose, ask yourself whether the map will be drawn for yourself or will it be shared? What will be easier to understand for others? Besides, a paper map is more personal and gives you more freedom for pictograms and layout, but it is less flexible to add branches. If the action of writing helps you learn and memorize better than typing, opt for a paper map. If you feel more comfortable with a very clearly structured document, go for a software. You will also notice that some softwares have designs similar to handwriting, making maps more personal.

Setting yourself limits... to identify the essential

To take advantage of mind mapping, you must learn to limit yourself. Two laws can guide you:

- **The Douglas Act**: The more space you have, the more you take up. Mind-mapping follows a tree-like structure and you could keep adding branches. Yet, your map could quickly become overloaded with information and be difficult to read. You can voluntarily limit the available space to make your map. For example, you can limit yourself to an A4 or A3 page to summarize a text of several pages. This will force you to focus on the relevant ideas as a priority.

- **Parkinson's Law**: The longer you have, the more time you will take. Making a mind map is akin to surfing the internet. You can spend hours and hours there. To avoid this pitfall, you must limit the time to make your map.

1.2.3 Choose your mind mapping software

There are plenty of mind-mapping softwares on the market. The choice will depend on several parameters:

- Your **needs**. What will be the purpose of your use? For brainstorming, most mind mapping softwares will do. If you want to write a full text, you must choose a software that can export to a word processor.

- Your **operating system** (Windows? Macintosh? Linux?). Some mind mapping softwares (such as Mindomo or MindMeister) are online services that do not require to be installed on your computer and do not depend on the operating system you use.

- Your **budget**. For tighter budgets, some mind mapping softwares are free. Others offer discounted licenses for students and academics.

- The **community** around the software. The broader and more active the community around it, the more you can exchange maps or even find help when needed.

For a good start we advise using XMind. It is a FreeMium licensed software. The basic version is free, the advanced features are part of a pay version. Below you will find a list of useful mind-mapping softwares. Check which one matches your criteria best.

SOFTWARE	Taking notes	Writing	Managing a project	Making a presentation	Collaborating
FreePlane / FreeMind	•	•	•		
XMind	•	•	•	•	•
MindManager	•	•	•	•	•
Ayoa	•	•		•	•
MindView	•	•	•	•	•

1.3 Memorize your notes

1.3.1 Discover how your memory works

We do not have one single memory, but several types which cooperate in the process of memorization. They can be classified in a time scale as follows:

- Sensory memory (a few milliseconds): we have a different type of memory for each sense (e.g. iconic memory for the sight, etc.).

- Short-term memory (less than a minute): It represents the short-term capacity of the brain. The work of the psychologist Miller showed that short-term memory could store 7 items in average. This may actually vary from 5 to 9 items (so 7 + 2 or 7-2) depending on the individual. You use this short-term memory when you recall the information you just heard from the teacher as you are taking notes.

- Long-term memory (from several minutes to several years): It also consists of several modules. In the context of your studies, two aspects will be particularly important: semantic memory and episodic memory.

    - Semantic memory, on the one hand, focuses on facts, meaning, concepts and knowledge from the external world. It enables to remember generic and context-free information and is not related to our own experience. It is abstract and involves verbal signals.

    - On the other hand, episodic memory, based on our own experience, sets events (from your personal experience) in a serial form. Time, places, are associated with emotions and specific contexts.

    - The semantic memory derives from the episodic memory, as we learn facts or concepts from our experiences.

1.3.2 Elaborate maps which are easy to remember

You will be able to memorize your mind-maps better and faster if you take the following elements into account:

- **Ranking**: you will remember information more easily if items are grouped together or classified in categories, especially if you are at the origin of this ranking. In a mind-map, you will classify information within a tree-shape. That is why it is better to create your own maps instead of memorizing ready-made ones. Indeed, the essential is not the map itself, but the whole process behind it: the creation, thinking and learning behind the map.

- **Images**: our brain memorizes images better than words. In your maps, express yourself as much as possible through pictograms or drawings.

- **Emotions**: Emotions strongly help the memorizing process. So, display emotions and feelings in your mind maps.

- **Helicopter view**: most people remember items better through a broad view or helicopter view than struggle with details. Mind-maps give a big picture and also enable to zoom in or out. When you zoom out, you focus on the information on the main branches and the main ideas and you get a helicopter view. When you zoom in on specific information, you concentrate on sub-branches and all the details.

- **Slicing-up information**: you cannot memorize and process heaps of information at one go. So do not overload a map. Instead, slice-up information, into several maps and sub-maps. Design a map that matches your short-term memorizing capacity, i.o.w do not exceed 5 to 9 main branches and 3 levels of sub-branches.

1.3.3 Memorize a map

To memorize a map, you should follow these steps:

- Step 1: Focus on the center.
- Step 2: Memorize the main branches, follow the clockwise direction. Start at the top right. Memorize the number of main branches. Then take the center as an axis of symmetry. Count the number of main branches to the right of the center then to the left.
- Step 3: Memorize the sub branches (of the main branches). Here again, follow the clockwise direction.
- Step 4: Try to do your memory map, then compare it with the original map.

Interview: Romain MARTYN

Biography: *Romain Martyn is a student at Kedge Business School, a business school that offers a master's degree in business engineering. "I discovered mind mapping quite young thanks to my uncle and have used it more and more over the years. I am also passionate about photography, skiing and the practice of apnea."*

1 - You have spent part of your education abroad in Canada and Finland. Is mind-mapping more widespread there?

In Canada, mind mapping is not so widespread, I have talked to a few professors and students. Although they were not familiar with this technique, they all reacted positively when I quickly explained the concept. Some students, on the other hand, were still wondering if it could be of any use to them and were not ready to change their habits. In Quebec, the educational system is different. Students must go through a Cégep, which is very similar to our IUTs (Institut Universitaire de Technologies - in France), in order to go to university. So, I guess it would have been different because I had never been told about mind mapping in high school either. As far as Finland is concerned, it is completely different. I have only been here for a month and I have realized that mind mapping is widespread, much more than in France for example. No teacher was surprised to see me take my notes with IMindMap (Ayoa), and we were given class documents in the form of map or even sketchnoting quite a few times. The most amazing thing is that there is a course for which I will be able to hand in the final assignment in the form of map, to the greater enjoyment of the teacher!

2 - How do you use mind mapping for your studies?

I use the mind mapping essentially for note-taking. This is more or less easy depending on the pedagogy of the teacher. For example, this is very handy when the plan is clear and there is a visual support like a PowerPoint on the board. It becomes a little less obvious to me when the course is only given orally. I also use mind mapping during exams or during the production of reports to build up my plan and visualize the main ideas before beginning to write.

3 - According to you, what are the advantages of mind mapping for a student?

Mind mapping has really made a difference in my studies. Most of all, it is time-saving. When I want to review or write a report, my notes are already synthesized and much more visual. Being able to see much more information on one page helps me to understand and remember faster. I also think of students who are used to taking all their courses on PDF or their notes to be able to do revision maps or summaries. As my notes are already in the shape of a map, everything is ready! The other thing that helps me a lot is that it is much more playful, when I take notes. I enjoy making a nice map with drawings, colors and small drawings. I find it more appealing than a Word document, for example, and I am convinced that having fun during the course helps me to remember everything I need.

CHAPTER 2:

READ AND TAKE NOTES WITH EFFICIENCY

Boost your reading skills!

Reading skills are an essential part of learning and a key tool for collecting, sorting and analyzing data. Improving these skills makes a major difference for students and life-long learners, especially in a world where infobesity (i.o.w information overload) and Internet are prominent.

Do technologies have an impact on our reading skills? As a language specialist, Maryanne Wolf (Tufts University) contrasts linear and non-linear approaches to reading (WOLF M. & BARZILLAI, 2009):

- In the traditional linear approach, one page follows the next, the text is split into paragraphs, and there are a limited number of images.

- For the non-linear approach, activated with Internet, there is a huge mass of information, hyperlinked text, videos alongside words and interactivity. To deal with this, Maryanne Wolf explains that our brains form shortcuts, all-scanning, searching for keywords, scrolling up and down quickly. Yet, there is growing evidence that it is more and more difficult for students to focus on longer, more complex texts. Maryanne Wolf suggests developing *bi-literate brains*, able to switch from one reading mode to the other.

- In the professional world, the same scanning strategy is used. You will seldom read a text entirely, but rather scan it to find a specific piece of information.

Moreover, texts are often considered as an end point, whose objective is to be understood or at best summarized. Let's turn them into a starting point considering reading as the beginning of deeper questions and never-before articulated thoughts.

To guide you along this journey, we will be developing three sets of tools for reading strategies:

- sustainable reading & thinking tools
- visual and mapping tools
- tips and insight to contrast reading on paper and on the web

To read and take notes with efficiency, students and life-long learners should be equipped with:

- Reading strategies, on the one hand: a first look at the text to get a general idea, the gist, followed by a more in-depth and detailed approach. This approach, also called skimming and scanning by some, is widespread in academic and learning contexts as well as in the media. Below you will find a few references of this skimming-scanning approach:
    - *The IELTS (International English Language Testing System) develops Reading, Scanning and reading for details.*

More information on: http://bit.ly/IELTS-Reading-SKills

- *The BBC, in the Skillswise section of their website, present the skim and scan technique. More information on http://bit.ly/BBC-Skimming*
- *The New-York Times: Skimming and Scanning: Using the New York Times to develop reading skills.*
  More information on: http://bit.ly/NYT-Skimming-and-Scanning

- Visual & Thinking tools on the other hand. The reading approach can be enhanced with a wide set of visual and thinking tools: mind-mapping, different types of maps and pictograms. These tools not only provide a quick access to information, as the brain processes images and structures faster than words, but it also supports the understanding, thinking and structuring processes.

To illustrate these reading strategies[1], we will analyze an article *Where gadgets go to die (2014)*, from the print press, namely from *The Economist.* It is a type of article that students would typically work and debate on. It belongs to the category of longer, *linear* article, split into clear-cut paragraphs and has very few images. It connects the themes of: electronic waste,

---

[1] The **reading strategies** developed in this booklet are based on the work of Professor J.P Callut.

the environment, and how rich and poor countries tackle waste treatment.

As shown in the map below, the first (quick) step to get a gist of a text will enable you to decide whether it is worth reading or not. The second step, in-depth reading, is devoted to *collecting* data. The third and last step will guide you through the process of creating *understanding maps,* which will bring you up to a deeper understanding of the text, making links between the different elements.

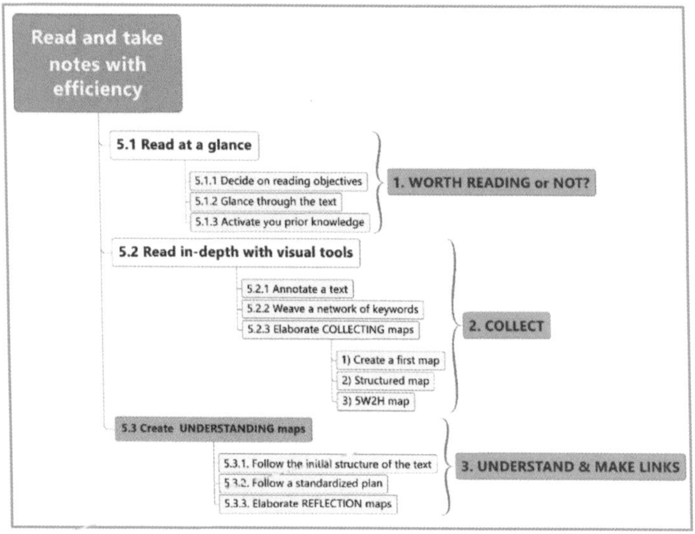

Fig. Roadmap of the chapter: 'Read and take notes with efficiency.'

Interview of Professor Jean-Paul Callut

What are reading strategies?

By reading comprehension strategies, we mean a set of approaches and techniques that allow the reader to gradually grasp the semantic structure of a text and to understand its content in more depth.

What are the benefits for students?

Reading comprehension strategies contribute to the acquisition and development of essential skills for the learner. Students learn how to:

- distinguish the essentials from the accessory
- identify difficulties in understanding and applying appropriate techniques to overcome them
- recognize the narrative structure of a text and represent it in the form of graphic organizers
- synthesize the content of the text.

What is your experience with reading strategies with students?

Learning these strategies and implementing them has enabled generations of students to become more autonomous, to "learn how to learn" and to broaden their mental horizons. They have acquired the desire to read more deeply.

Writing for the web ... to help read better.

Reading a linear text on paper differs broadly from reading a hyperlinked text online. You should know that:

- Reading online is 25 % slower than on paper.[2]
- Online readers automatically skim and scan a text online, picking out the keywords or heading of their choice. In addition, they extract only the information they are interested in, ignoring other material.

Consequently, a good web writer must adapt his writing technique to help the reader.

Web writers make extensive use of:

- bullet-points
- words in **bold**
- varied levels of headings
- a pyramidal structure that guides the reader from the most important information to the least important one. Often, the beginning of an article follows the 5W+2H approach; i.e, the very beginning of the text answers the questions: *who, what, where, when, why* and *how, how much*. The

[2]These figures are put forward by Jacob Nielsen (1999) and are often given as a reference for the speed of reading on the web. Judy Gregory (2004).

rest of the text usually provides less relevant information.

Besides, the first readers on the web are search engines. The web writer thus involves in a dialogue with a robot! As the aim is to be listed at the top of the search pages, the web writer reiterates the same keywords over and over again, avoiding rich and varied vocabulary, an academic style as well as wordplays.

Furthermore, it is easier to take notes from a text online than on paper. Indeed, a text on the web is often structured with subtitles. Yet, you can easily get lost in the maze of links and hyperlinks on the web; and it can prove to be tricky to identify the best page for a topic.

2.1 Read for gist

2.1.1 Decide on reading objectives

Before reading, make sur you set clear objectives and answer the following questions:

- Why are you reading this text, for which purpose?
- What type of information are you looking for?
- Is a quick overview of the text enough or do you need additional details?
- How much time can you devote to this reading task?

Bear in mind that you may take the liberty to focus on one part only, or on tracking only specific elements or themes. At each stage, you have the possibility to read further or to interrupt if the text doesn't match your objectives. It is thus essential to set clear reading goals and to follow them. Adjust the time spent on each part in line with your objectives.

- The reading objective we have set for the article *Where gadgets go to die,* is to read and take notes with efficiency, in order to be ready to summarize the text. This objective is fairly general and is a typical exercise for academic skills. Your reading objective could be more targeted, of course.

2.1.2 Glance through a text

Glancing through a text is the very first step of the process and the quickest one. It shouldn't take more than an average of ten to fifteen minutes for a text of one to two pages. This may vary depending on the length of the text.

Follow these steps:

1. **Identify the structure**: Start by analyzing the title and subtitle of the text. They should encompass the main ideas. What information can you learn from the table of contents (if any), the illustrations and graphs?

2. **Look at the metadata**: What about the author, his position, the type of publication (book, review...), the date, the source.

3. **Read the beginning and the end of the text**: Read the introduction and conclusion of the text. Then, read the first and last line of each paragraph (or chapters if you are reading a book). Which keywords stand out? Does it support the elements you found in the

title/subtitle? Take quick notes of these elements, maybe in the margin of the text.

We also recommend to make a first map with your findings, either a pen-and-paper one or using a mapping software.

2.1.3 Activate your prior knowledge

Now that you have extracted raw ideas from the text, it is time to activate your prior knowledge. You can start by brainstorming on the content of the text. If you possess no prior knowledge on the topic, you may skip this step.

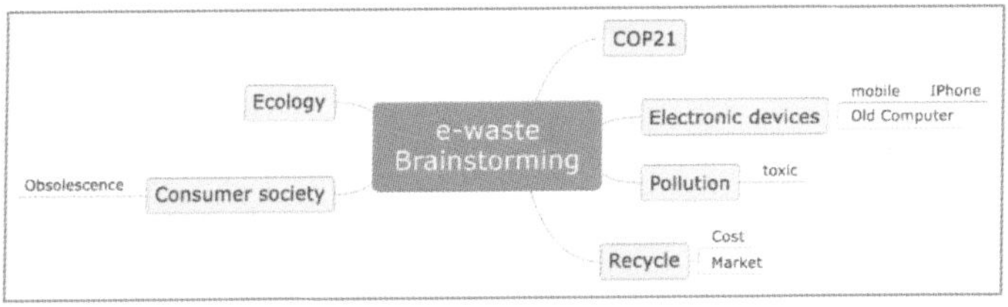

Fig: Brainstorming on the main themes of the article Where gadgets go to die.

A very convenient way to make sure you have explored all necessary items of your prior knowledge, is to use the 5W-2H method, which is an immediate and comprehensive way to collect information. You may need to use another structure to organize the data collected afterwards, though. Yet, it is an excellent beginning.

The 5W-2H questions are:

What ? Who ? When ? Where ? Why ?	How ? How much?

Draw a map with each question on each branch and try to complete the map with answers. You may as well work on your previous brainstorming map. Some questions may remain unanswered. List the questions in the order that suits you best. You may also complete this map throughout the reading process as some elements will only emerge progressively. You will often notice that the answers to the questions *Why?* and *How?* stand out.

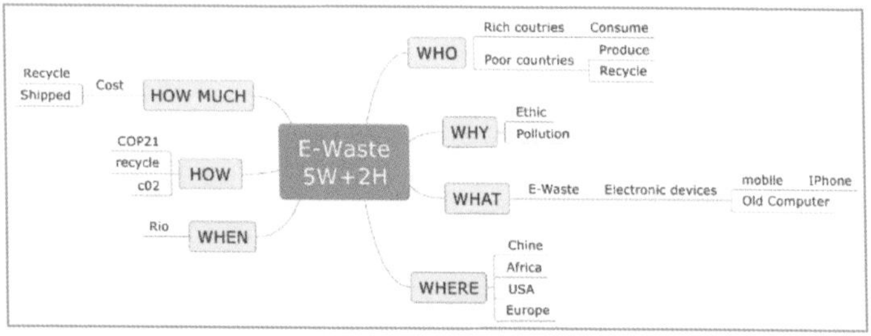

Fig: 5W-2H map for a comprehensive exploration of a topic

2.2 Read in-depth and map with visual tools

The scanning phase is devoted to collecting the necessary data.

2.2.1 Annotate a text visually

This raises three issues:

1. How to identify essential information?
2. How to identify keywords and linking words?
3. How to display information visually?

As a first step, highlight the extracts of the text you consider relevant.

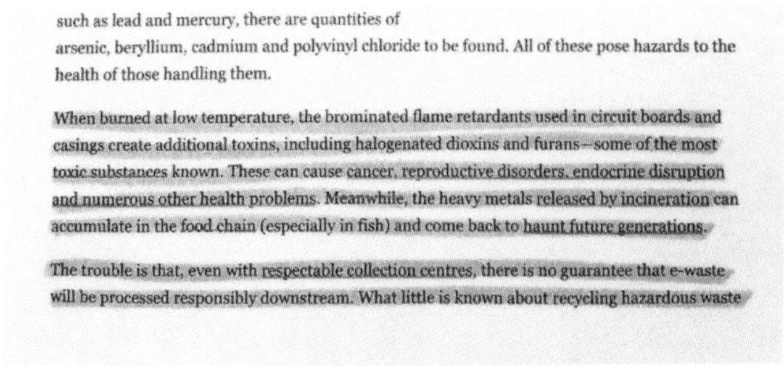
such as lead and mercury, there are quantities of arsenic, beryllium, cadmium and polyvinyl chloride to be found. All of these pose hazards to the health of those handling them.

When burned at low temperature, the brominated flame retardants used in circuit boards and casings create additional toxins, including halogenated dioxins and furans—some of the most toxic substances known. These can cause cancer, reproductive disorders, endocrine disruption and numerous other health problems. Meanwhile, the heavy metals released by incineration can accumulate in the food chain (especially in fish) and come back to haunt future generations.

The trouble is that, even with respectable collection centres, there is no guarantee that e-waste will be processed responsibly downstream. What little is known about recycling hazardous waste

Fig. Highlight all the important passages in the text.

Throughout the in-depth reading phase, you are liable to take notes. Keeping your reading objectives in mind, you may either annotate the text itself, create a map directly, or combine both. The margin will be a very precious space for your comments.

Moreover, the use of pictograms can be helpful. They provide a very quick gateway to information and function as visual tags and help trace information and find it back quickly. Just as you see signposts along the road as you drive, pictograms signpost the path of ideas. Yet, many people aren't used to drawing pictograms. In fact, they do not require any artistic talent. The simplest, quickest and clearest, the most efficient. Basic shapes as lines, circles, squares and triangles will be the starting point to sketch objects, concepts, actions, emotions ... Stick figures or stars are a handy way to draw people's attention. You can also think of designing pictograms to signpost the text, to indicate if you need to take action (e.g: checking a source, investigating one element further) ...

Fig: Examples of pictograms

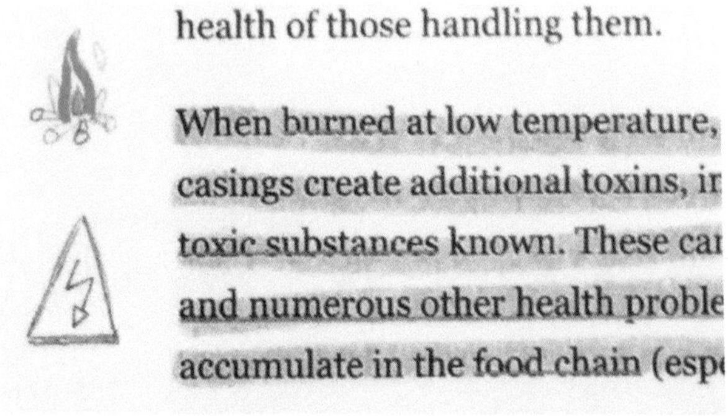

health of those handling them.

When burned at low temperature, casings create additional toxins, ir toxic substances known. These car and numerous other health proble accumulate in the food chain (esp

Fig: Annotate the text with pictograms

To keep track of this *visual language*, keep a notebook with all your pictograms. Little by little, you will enrich it and elaborate your own visual directory (on paper or digital).

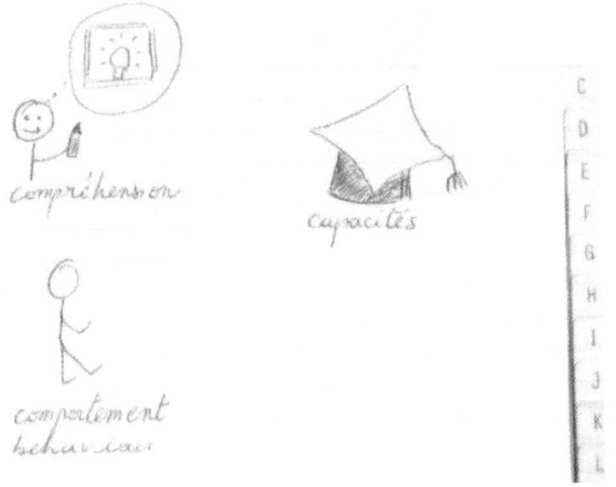

Fig: Elaborate a visual directory by keeping a notebook with your pictograms

2.2.2 Weave a web of keywords and connectives

As you are reading a text in-depth, start tracking keywords, and connectives (Connective are all linking words (prepositions, conjunctions, adverbs) that help to structure a text and make links). For the analysis of the article *Where gadgets go to die*, we have chosen two visually distinct forms:

- a **circular capsule** for connectives and guiding language,
- a **squared capsule** for keywords.

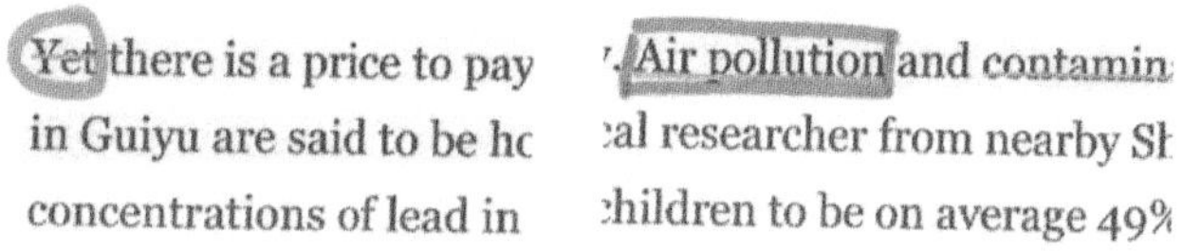
Yet there is a price to pay
in Guiyu are said to be hc
concentrations of lead in

'. Air pollution and contamin
:al researcher from nearby Sh
:hildren to be on average 49%

Fig: Circular capsules for connectives and squared capsule for keywords

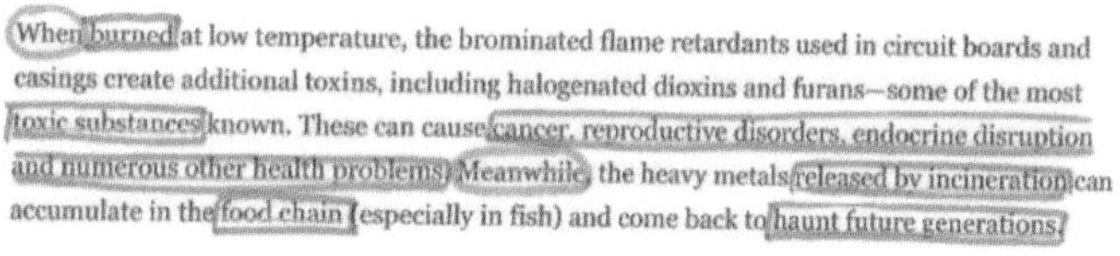
When burned at low temperature, the brominated flame retardants used in circuit boards and casings create additional toxins, including halogenated dioxins and furans—some of the most toxic substances known. These can cause cancer, reproductive disorders, endocrine disruption and numerous other health problems. Meanwhile, the heavy metals released by incineration can accumulate in the food chain (especially in fish) and come back to haunt future generations.

Fig: Connectives and keywords

Keywords convey essential information about the text, which will be useful to summarize it later. Connectives and signaling devices help display the structure and order of ideas in a text. If well-used, they are equivalent to the backbone of a text.

Connectives can express time, comparison and contrast, reason and result, purpose, condition, opinion, adding and summarizing. The following document is a recap of common connectives, classified by their meaning and the grammatical category they belong to. (CALLUT, 2015).

CONNECTIVES	CONJUNCTIONS	PREPOSITIONS	ADVERBS
Time	When While As soon as Before After Since Until/til As long as Whenever	During Before After Since Until/till	Meanwhile, After that, Afterwards, Then, First, Firstly
Comparison & Contrast	Although Though Even though Whereas While Otherwise Or else	In spite of Despite Instead of	However, Yet, Still, Nevertheless, Instead, On the one hand, on the other hand On the contrary, Otherwise, Or else,
Reason & Result	Because As / since Seeing that So that	Due to Owing to Because of Thanks to	That's why So, As a result, Therefore, Consequently,
Purpose	(not) to In order (not) to So as (not) to		
Condition	If / in case Provided that As long as Unless		
Opinion			Actually, in fact, As far as I'm concerned, For my part, In my opinion, In my view, In any case, At any rate, Anyway, Obviously, That's all very well but... Too bad! So what? However that may be, Definitely.
Adding something		In addition (to that), ... As well as...	In addition (to that), ... Besides, ... Moreover, ... Furthermore, ...
Summarizing		In brief, briefly... In a few words, ... In short, ... To cut a long story short, ... In conclusion, ... In a nutshell, ...	

How to identify essential information?

➠ The Pareto Principle:

The Pareto principle (AZAD, K.), introduced by the Italian economist Vilfredo Pareto at the end of the 19th century, is an empirical phenomenon which can be observed in various fields: 80 % of the effects come from 20 % of the causes. If we were to apply it to reading strategies, it would mean that 20 % of the text conveys 80 % of its message.

➠ Newspaper blackout:

Thanks to his work as an artist and author, Austin Kleon, opens up an alternative way to identifying essential information in a text. In the video *How to make a newspaper blackout poem*, he puts the following technique forward: get a newspaper and some markers, pick a section and an article, box the words you like, and blackout the words you don't need. (KLEON, 2015) By crossing out all superfluous information and colouring it black, the reader is left with the meaningful elements only. What about transposing this technique to reading strategies?

➠ Primacy and recency effects

The first and last elements of a series are crucial and are remembered better than elements standing in the middle. Pay a specific attention to the beginning and end of a paragraph, a text, a chapter or a book.

It is also easier to memorize elements, which are repetitive, extraordinary or when information is put into a context.

Stick to your reading objectives

The closer you stick to your objectives, the easier it will be to identify what you are looking for.

2.2.3 Elaborate a collecting map

Once you have finished scanning and encapsulating, take a separate piece of paper and start spreading the keywords around the title or main theme of the text in a circular way.

Below you will find examples of:

- a first map based on the keywords of *Where gadgets go to die*. The keywords are displayed around the title.
- You will then find a structured map, in which the keywords have been grouped together by meaning.
- Finally, you will find a map based on a 5W2H structure.

1) Create a first map, on software or on paper.

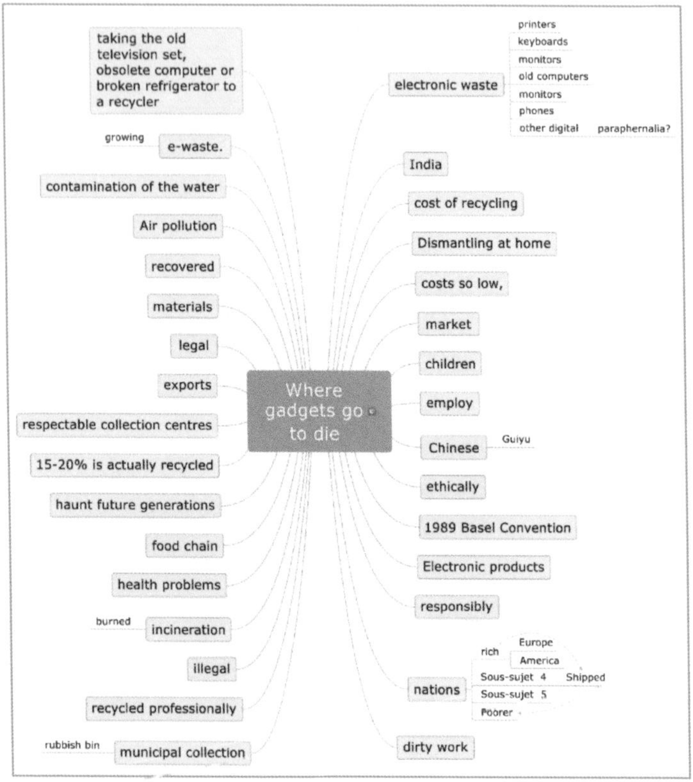

Fig: First map with the keywords of the article, done with the software XMind.

2) Structured map

You can also group keywords together in a structured map.

Visual notes can be taken on the text itself or if needed on a separate piece of paper. How detailed should these notes be? It all depends on the objectives you have set at the beginning.

For some texts, visual signposts in the margin will be enough. For others, it is worth taking distance from the text, reorganizing the ideas and displaying them in various types of maps.

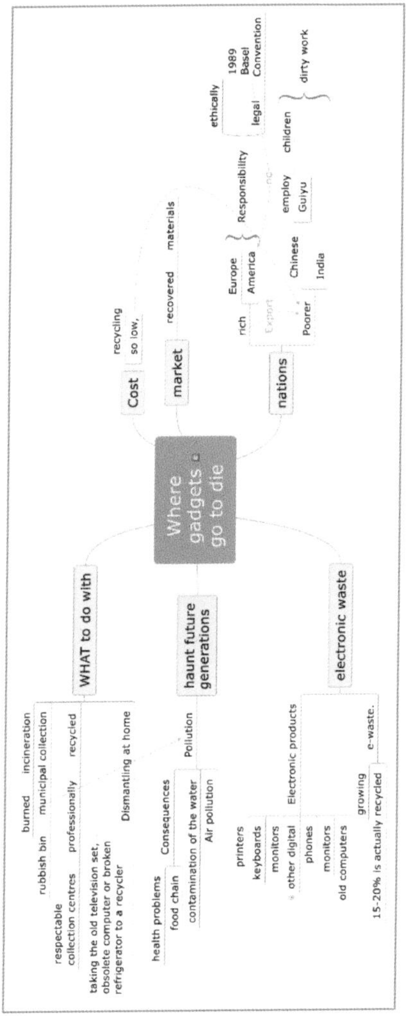

Fig: The data from the first webbing has been re-organized and completed.

3) 5W2H map

The 5W2H layout, introduced at the beginning of the chapter for data collection can be used again at different stages of the process.

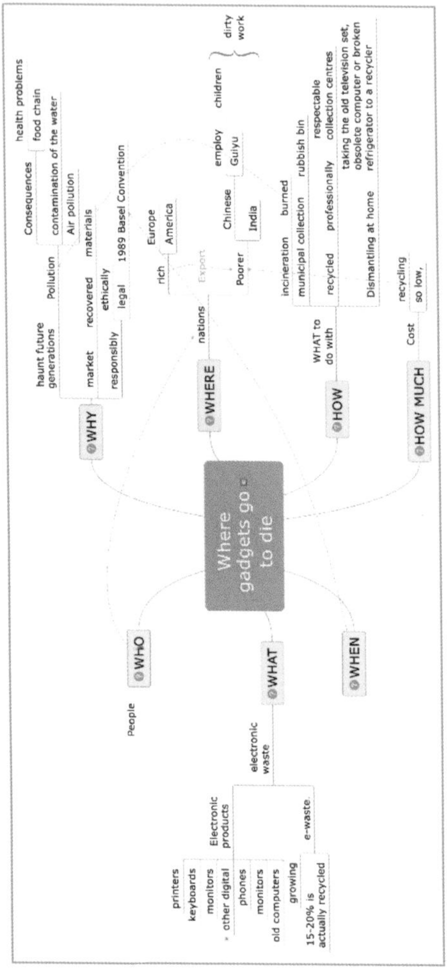

Fig: Map re-structured on the basis of the 5W-2H questions, which may come up at different stages of the process.

This 5W2H structure serves as an intermediate plan. It will make essential ideas emerge. Yet, you may not be able to answer all questions, and they may not all be relevant.

Map easily and quickly with a webbing, a technique developed by Gabriele Rico.

This visual tool was first developed by Gabriele Rico in her doctoral dissertation at Stanford in 1976 and was spread through her book *Writing The Natural Way* (1984).

How to proceed? First, note down the topic at the centre of the page, write down the essential keywords and concepts of the text around it. Encapsulate each word. Then, as a second step, indicate links and relationships between the ideas with arrows and lines. If needed, erase and reposition the capsules (DELENGAIGNE, 2011).

Webbing and mind-mapping are often confused. Mind-mapping has a well-designed tree structure, makes use of keywords and drawings or pictograms. Webbing has a more creative approach, is less structured, and functions with keywords only (it has no or few images).

Fig. Hand-drawn webbing with the keywords of the text Where gadgets go to die

2.3 Create understanding maps

This third and last step will guide you through the process of creating *understanding maps,* which will bring you up to an in-depth understanding of the text, making links between its different elements.

To summarize with a map, you should:

- follow the text,
- reorganize information into a standardized plan
- design a visual display of your own.

2.3.1 Follow the initial structure of the text

Depending on your objectives and on the text, you may choose to reproduce the initial plan of the text. The paragraphs, or main parts or titles of the text may then become the main branches of your map.

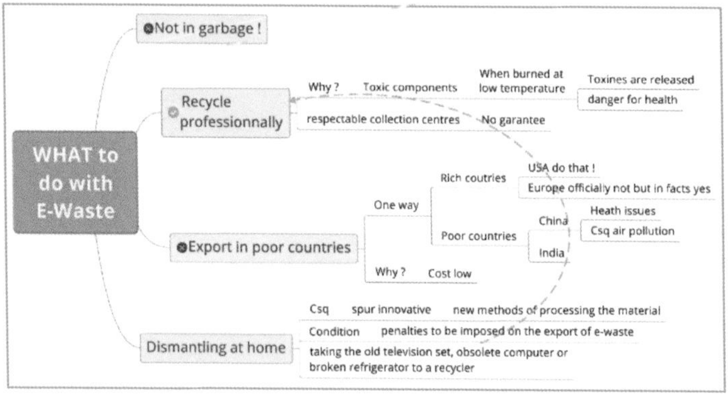

Fig. Map following the initial structure of the text

In *Where Gadgets go to die*, there are few indications of subtitles, and, at times, it appears difficult to follow the backbone of the text.

2.3.2 Follow a standardized plan

If you hesitate on where to start with the analysis, the two methods below are very effective to have ideas emerge from a text:

- **Thesis - Antithesis - Synthesis:**

This plan is widely used to answer questions of the type: "Discuss the following point of view...". The thesis presents a viewpoint or opinion. The antithesis shows that the original thesis is incomplete or contradictory. The synthesis "enables to go beyond the conflict raised" (FRANCESCHI 2003). The synthesis indeed brings a resolution of the conflict by identifying common elements and forming a new proposition.

The philosopher Hegel significantly contributed to the use of this mode of thinking. To him, everything originated in conflicting opposites, which are then reconciled to form a new element.

- **SPRI**

The SPRI method was developed by Louis Timbal Duclaux, who has focused on professional (and creative) writing throughout his career in French energy companies (TIMBAL-DUCLAUX, 1983). SPRI stands for Situation, Problem, Resolution and Information. It is a very efficient way of structuring ideas and information around a problem-solving case.

Even if it is primarily a thinking tool, it can easily be displayed visually into a mind-map with four main branches. Complete the branches with Situation, Problem, Resolution and Information. If the text raises more than one problem, add branches as needed.

To implement it, follow the guidelines below:

- Situation: Explain the situation, providing enough context to have a broad view, as if you were explaining it to someone who is new to the topic.

- Problem: Present it as a critical question, a real obstacle, not a mere abstract question. Be sure to articulate the problem in a clear and logical way.

- Resolution: Recap the principles of the solution. Further details will be supplied below.

- Information: Detail the principles outlined in the solution. Provide all the details and practical aspects needed. The *Information* part is optional.

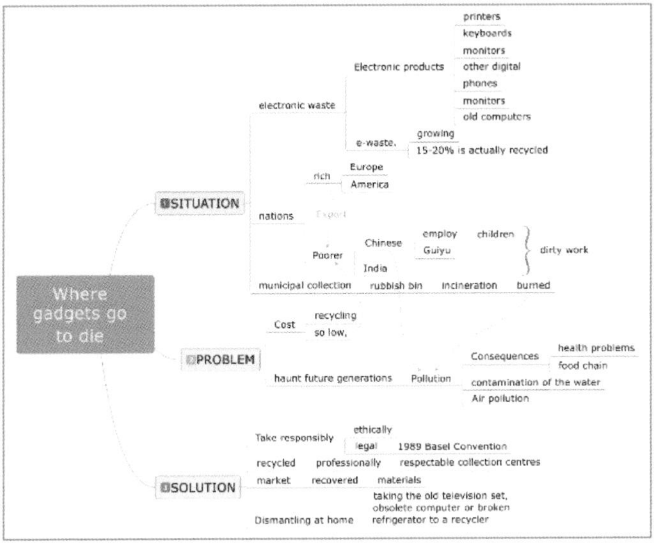

Fig: Summary of Where gadgets go to die in a SPR(I) structure

2.3.3 Elaborate reflection maps

The last option is to take distance from the text, and keeping your objectives in mind, design a structure to make it your own.

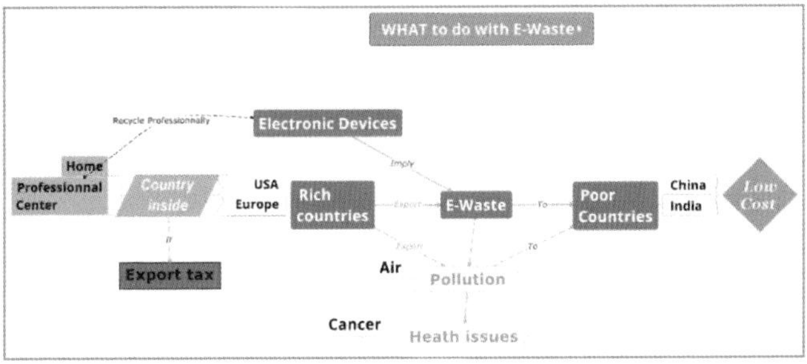

Fig a.: Map with a design and structure of your own.

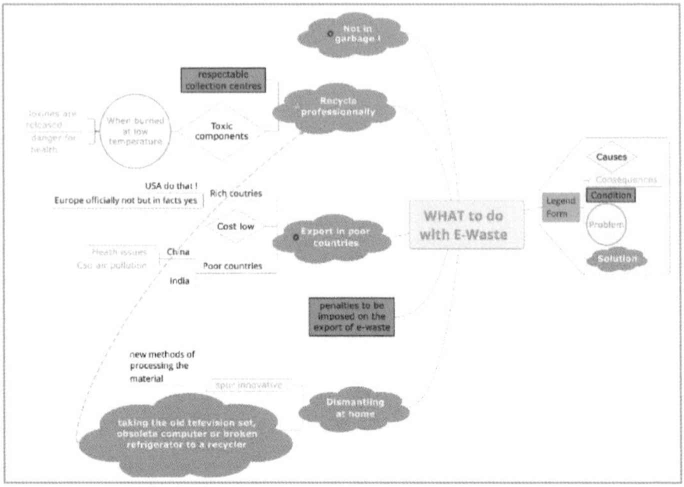

Fig b: In this map, each shape refers to a clear meaning.

This map even goes a step beyond. It could be depicted as a *systemic map.* Its aim is:

- to highlight the links between the concepts and elements of the text
- to display at the same time a global as well as a detailed view
- to provide a specific meaning for each shape.

Indeed,

- the diamond-shape refers to causes
- the parallelogram refers to consequences
- the circle refers to problems
- the cloud refers to solutions

The two maps above take distance from the layout of typical mind-maps. They dig deeply into displaying the interaction and hierarchy of ideas. The systemic map integrates all elements of the text and plays with shapes bearing a specific meaning.

Reading strategies with the mapping software XMind.

XMind is an excellent companion for reading strategies: not only does the software enable to make a wide range of maps (mind-mapping, the cause / consequence Ishikawa fishbone chart, timelines…), but it also provides a convenient way of classifying and displaying the different steps of the reading process.

XMind is structured into sheets that can be added and linked into one document.

Start by creating a central map or "master map" and link it to secondary maps. The secondary maps depict objectives, the skimming and scanning phases, and additional maps developed throughout the analysis. You can also add links to relevant websites or documents.

How to deal with information overload?

Up to now, the common response to information accumulating has been to increase data storage, often in computer files, which become massive. Yet, this will not be manageable in the long run. It is thus essential to find another way of coping with this phenomenon. In his book *Things that make us smart*, Donald Norman puts forward the idea of turning data into a FLOW of information (NORMAN, 1993).

The recommendation when dealing with a big amount of data is being able to track back information at the moment you need it. Furthermore, there is more than one way to access numerical data. Tag documents carefully, have one code per project.

Data is physically in one location but accessing it may come from different paths or different combinations of tags. You may use Evernote to collect information and classify it. In your tags, try to include at least two elements for your documents: *what?* And *why?* In order to cross different sources of information.

CHAPTER 3:

TAKE NOTES DURING LESSONS

After having discovered mind mapping as well as tools and techniques to read and take notes with efficiency, let us focus on another note-taking method during lessons, from an oral source.

3.1 Listen actively

3.1.1 Know your note-taking profile

Before you go into practical aspects of note-taking, take a step back to reflect on how your understanding process operates. Jean-François Michel distinguishes three types of *understanding* profiles and outlines the implications for note-taking (MICHEL, 2005).

- AUDITIVE students understand through LISTENING. For those students, it is thus essential to be in a quiet part of the room and be able to give all the attention required to what the teacher is saying. After the lesson, ask yourself: "Can I explain what I heard?"

- VISUAL students understand through what is seen: images, graphs, structures, diagrams, After the lesson, ask yourself: Am I able to sketch, draw, represent what has been said?

- KINESTHETIC understand through what is felt. Students learn/understand better by doing. After the lesson, ask yourself: "Can I find a concrete example / a case to enabling me to explain what I heard.

To help you determine your learning profile, surf on : https://www.apprendreaapprendre.com/tests/

It has often been argued that labeling learners or students with a clearly determined profile may be excessive. Let us just take this as a guideline and acknowledge that learners may have a dominant profile, and secondary skills as well.

3.1.2 Anticipate (exam) questions.

The more prepared you are when you walk into a classroom for a lecture, the easiest it will be to process information. Table of contents, coursebooks, plannings can already guide you. Activate your prior knowledge as well. Writing down a set of open and closed questions will set your brain on an active mode. The more you get accustomed to it, the easier it will be to come up with relevant questions. Your objective during the lesson, of course, will be to answer them or to determine whether they lead to other questions.

- For open questions (what, why, how...), you expect to obtain broad (and open) answers
- Closed questions will be answered by a yes, no or precise elements such as when, how much.

You will find out that questions are powerful tools to support your listening and understanding skills.

Your questions and note-taking style will vary from one subject to the other. Some lessons are based on chronology, facts, events and the way events are linked, others on communicative skills, thinking skills, problem-solving. Of course, choose the right type of questions for each course.

To come up with relevant questions, do not hesitate to transpose the SQ3R (Survey, Question, Read, Recite, Review) reading Technique to note-taking in class. The SQ3R method is a five-step process, developed by an educational psychologist Francis Pleasant Robinson for college students to help the brain focus on a specific goal and to become active in the learning process by raising and answering questions. When you read a text or open a textbook for the first time, you should transform titles or subtitles into questions (open or closed questions). The lecture will be dedicated to identifying elements to answer them.

A winning strategy is to put yourself into your teacher's shoes and imagine which questions could come up up the exam. At the end of each chapter, draw a list of potential exam questions.

3.1.3 Identify the structure and key ideas

- Identify the structure

Being able to identify the structure of the course is an essential tool to support your understanding, and later your memorizing process. For some lessons, the structure is clear. For others, it may take more time for it to emerge, or you may have to elaborate your own structure. By coming up with a structure of your own, you also demonstrate that you have gained a deep understanding of a topic.

Obviously, your starting point will be the table of contents from your lesson or textbook. Refer to it frequently. You should also take some time and distance to reflect upon the links between the different parts.

- Identify key ideas

Taking notes of every single word you hear is almost impossible. The process of note-taking already implies processing the information you hear by selecting and organizing information. Based on the structure you have elaborated previously (or are still elaborating) complete with key ideas, and then examples or demonstrations. Leave blanks if you missed out some information, to complete later on.

3.2 Take notes

To illustrate the listening and note-taking strategies, we will analyze the lesson from Scott Galloway, Professor of Marketing at NYU Stern School of Business. The general topic is the following: *"In the race for digital dominance, the Gang of Four have emerged - Amazon, Facebook, Google, and Apple. As they continue to grab share in the retail and media industries, who will fall victim at the hands of the gang? What are their impacts on broader business and society as a whole? Scott Galloway, FTMBA 92, Clinical Professor of Marketing at the NYU Stern School of Business and Founder of L2, outlines his predictions in a 90-mile-an-hour volley of data and insights."* (GALLOWAY, 2017) Click on the following link to listen to this lecture: http://bit.ly/tedtalkGalloway

3.2.1 Take note with the Cornell method

The Cornell method is a system for taking, organizing and reviewing notes that was developed by Prof. Walter Paulk at Cornell university.

How to proceed?

To start with, write down the course title, date and page number at the top of your sheet. Then, divide your page in 3 sections:

1- Notes section (during the lesson)

During the lesson, take notes and focus on keywords, eliminate unnecessary information. Use symbols and abbreviations. Leave enough space between the items or paragraphs, in order to complete your notes afterwards.

In the review phase, you should keep this column for examples.

2- Cues section (after the lesson)

Pull out the key points from your notes (key ideas, people, dates, definitions…). Use pictograms, symbols to tag information. It will be quicker to track it and find it back. You can also write down questions that help connect different elements.

This column should be studied and known extremely well.

3- Summary section (after the lesson)

In the bottom section, you should write a concise review of the essential ideas from the page.

CORNELL NOTES

<table>
<tr><td rowspan="2">Cues Section

(after the lesson)
Key points & ideas
People / dates / definitions</td><td>Course Title</td><td>Date
Page number</td></tr>
<tr><td colspan="2">Take notes

(during the lesson) Take notes. Focus on keywords. Eliminate unnecessary nformation. Use symbols and abbreviations. Write down (some) examples.</td></tr>
<tr><td colspan="3">Summary

(after the lesson) Concise review of the essential ideas from the page</td></tr>
</table>

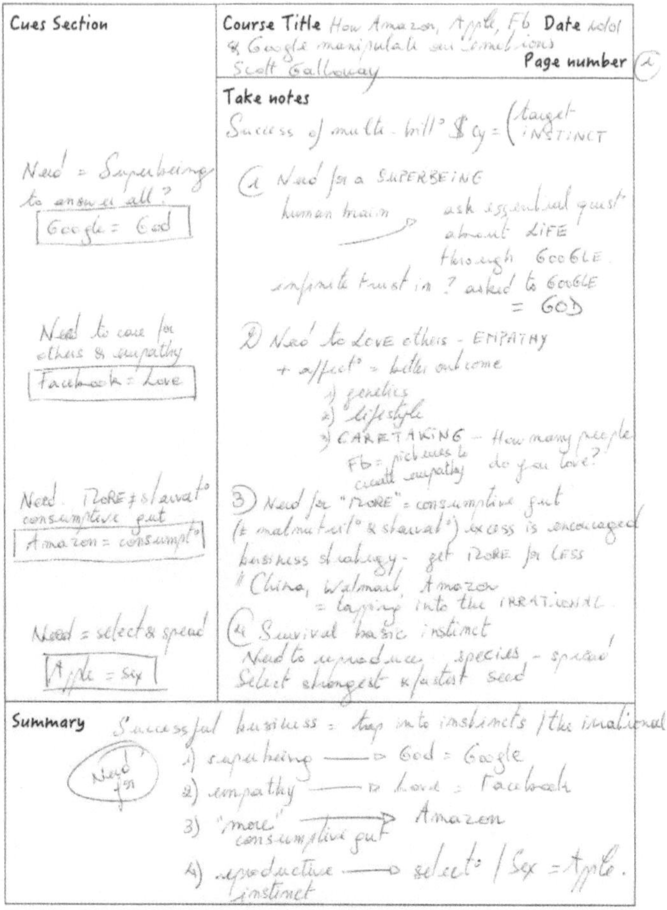

Fig. Taking notes with the Cornell method, based on Scott Galloway's lecture.

3.2.2 Make your notes visual and simple to memorize

In the previous chapter, we saw how to annotate a text visually. The same is true for note-taking. Pictograms, symbols, arrows, help sign out your notes. Visual elements can be drawn during the note-taking phase or afterwards.

Sketchnote your program

Sketchnoting is a visual note-taking technique that provides less constraints than mind-mapping. It combines both sketching and note-taking (sketch + note). Developed by Mike Rhode in 2010, it enables to memorize better, enjoy note-taking itself and synthesize information. (DELENGAIGNE 2017) Indeed sketchnoting does not require a fixed tree-shape structure with branches and gives more freedom to display information. Besides, sketchnotes can contain mind maps. In the pictures below, the program of one term is summarized in a sketchnote.

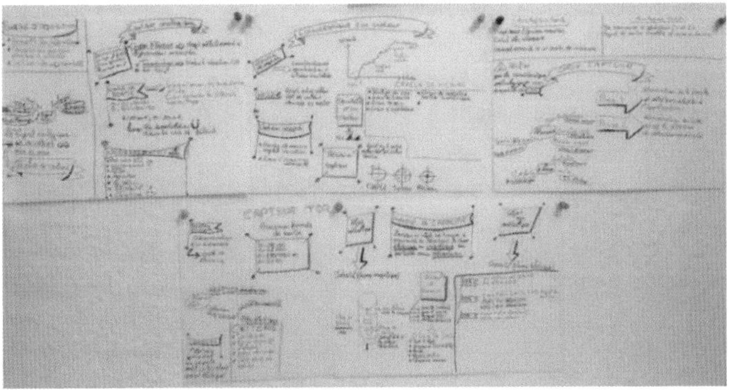

Program of one semester: Romain MARTYN

3.2.3 Take notes with a pen or a keyboard?

Do you prefer taking notes with a computer or with pen and paper? It is becoming more common to see rows of students behind laptop screens. Before you make a choice, let us weigh the two options.

- Many students type faster than they write. So, obviously, a computer could be a good option. In addition, a study shows that students manage to write words verbatim, i.e, transcribing exactly the same words. Their notes are thus more complete and are very close to what the lecturer says during the lecture. (MUELLER, P. A. & OPPENHEIMER, D.M. 2014)

- Yet, writing out notes by hand, according to the same study, fosters memorizing factual details, understanding the concepts of a lesson and the ability to synthesize. Indeed, as writing happens slower, it forces the student to capture essential information and to process it before writing it down. The brain is highly active throughout these operations. With verbatim note-taking on a computer, students focus on what they hear and transcribe it, without necessarily understanding it.

- This, of course, excludes the distraction created by notifications, instant mails, applications, social networks , which may take up to 40% of the attention during the time spent in class, according to the same study, disrupting heavily the attention capacity.

- Which conclusion should be drawn? Should note-taking with a computer be avoided or banned? Students should certainly be warned about its downsides. No matter what, the number of students using their laptops keeps increasing and technology is affecting our brains in unexpected ways.

Case study: Taking note with One Note, from Microsoft

Keeping all these cognitive downsides in mind, it is worth exploring the benefits of some digital note-taking solutions. Microsoft One Note is a popular one among students. It enables to organize notes, research documents and material. You may also include a variety of sources: text, pictures, digital handwriting, audio, access internet. There is also a sharing mode in order to work collaboratively. These features set note-taking in another dimension. Yet, the objective should remain clear, and all the sources of information from the course should be synthesized, at some point. Mind mapping can bring a positive contribution in that respect.

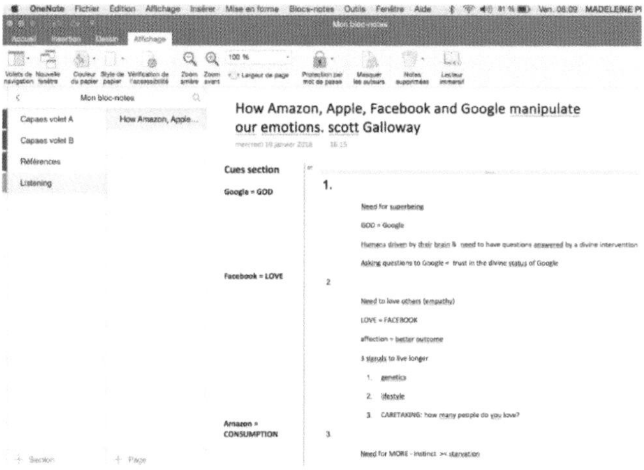

Fig : Note-taking with One Note. it is also possible to add text boxes in order to combine with Cornell Notes.

3.3 Take notes with mind mapping

3.3.1 Listen and process information differently with mind mapping

In the chapter **Discover mind mapping**, you explored mind-maps thanks to which information is displayed in a tree-like shape, rather than a linear one. Mind mapping is a very active process for the brain which involves a series of learning gestures: listening or paying attention, memorizing, understanding, thinking and imagining. With an optimal note-taking strategy, these can happen alltogether (LE BIHAN, AMBROSINI, EICHENLAUB, DE LARDEMELLE & PAILLEAU, 2012.) Note-taking is indeed the main access to the content that should be understood, remembered and thought about with imagination.

This tree-like view fosters

- link-making
- identifying common or opposed elements
- understanding
- memorizing
- thinking.

Indeed, in contrast to linear note-taking, mind mapping:

- shows the connections and the hierarchies between ideas
- provides a broad and generic view of a topic
- encourages to write down fewer but more meaningful words (focusing on key-words and key-ideas)

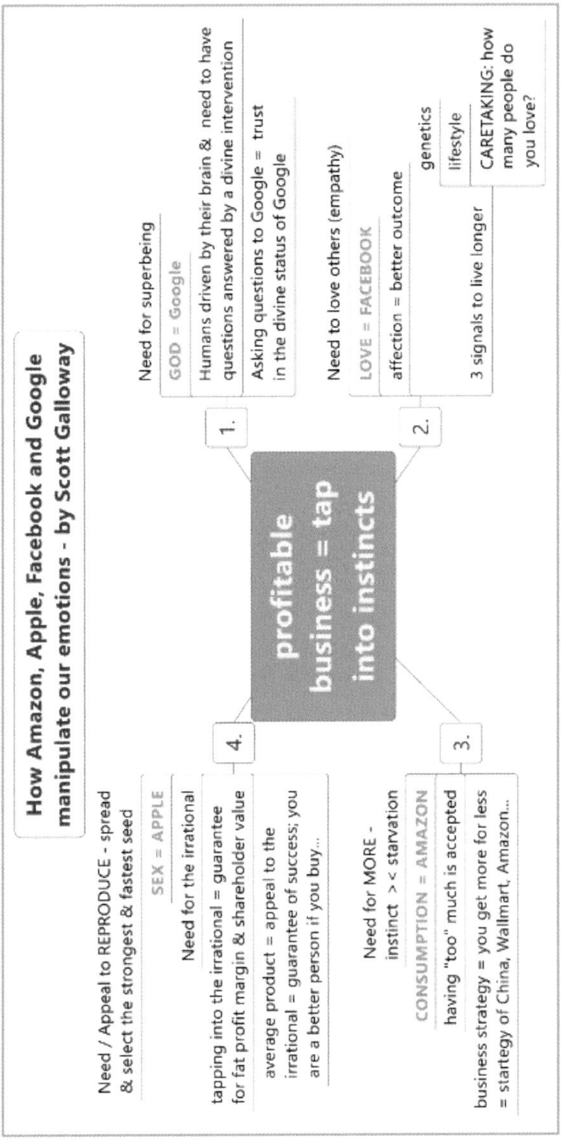

Fig: Mind map of "How Amazon, Apple, Facebook and Google manipulate our emotions" by Scott Galloway.

3.3.2 Take notes in class

Taking notes in class or at a conference is a challenging task which would require to map either faster or as fast as writing. Yet, for that precise reason, it prompts a slightly different attitude. It compels the note-taking to increase the level of attention as fewer words or phrases are written down, yet more meaningful ones. It also pushes the mapper to understand what is heard and to make links between ideas.

These elements may also be present in linear note-taking, of course. Mind mapping, though, does not leave a choice. Mapping forces the listener to go one step further in the process of learning, thinking and memorizing.

If you are ready for a try, here are a few tips to make note-taking with mind-maps smoother during class:

1) Before class:

- to be well-prepared and already have an idea of what will be dealt with.
- prepare a map of the table of contents or of the plan of the lesson beforehand, if possible. Mapping the table of contents of a course is a powerful tool, that will help you navigate between the ideas.
- sketch some maps for the main parts, leaving plenty of space to complete it during the lesson.

2) During class:

- pay (very) close attention

3) After class

- finalize the aesthetic aspect of your map: illustrate it with pictograms and add colors.
- take some distance and thinking time to use your imagination and create even more or unexpected links between the ideas.
- complete your map with additional information or further references if needed.

3.3.3 Synthetize your notes

Are your notes ready to be used as learning material? Depending on the requirements for the course, you may limit yourself to the notes taken in class, or, more commonly, you will have to compile a series of documents: notes from class, the powerpoint presentation of the teacher, additional readings, essays or research done for the course.

It may indeed require time to transform and synthesize the different documents into the final version of the study material. Ideally, this study material should be ready before the revision period. Mind mapping is an effective tool when it comes to synthesizing, whether notes are taken in a linear structure, with Cornell notes or with a mind map.

The benefit of a synthesis in mind-mapping is :

- to give a helicopter view of a topic by zooming out, enabling to make links between ideas and elements.
- to give a detailed view of the topic, by zooming into the map.
- to make it easier to understand the topic
- to contribute to the understanding, memorizing and thinking processes.

CONCLUSION

We hope this journey through mind mapping, reading, listening and note taking strategies will contribute to a more efficient and successful way of learning. Taking notes (with mind mapping) doesn't end with your studies, though. It is a lifelong process which will carry on during meetings, at conferences and throughout your career. Adopting lifelong study tools (as mind mapping) will help you cope with a professionally fast changing environment.

Mind mapping is not limited to taking notes. You can use it in your professional and personal life to manage a project, to conduct a brainstorming, to make a presentation and much more.

Furthermore, by applying Mc Luhan's principle (*The tools we use shape our thinking)* to mind mapping, we can clearly see that the essential is not the information conveyed in our maps, but the way mind mapping shapes our way of thinking, our behaviour, the way our ideas are structured. In other words, using calculation spreadsheets extensively will bring you to think *in a grid*. Using mind mapping will boost your creativity! So have fun with mind mapping and enjoy this lifelong tool to read, listen, take notes and much more.

Give yourself time, though, as mind mapping (and new tools) require practice and see you soon to share the benefits you will have reaped from mind mapping.

Bibliography

Azad, K. Understanding the Pareto Principle. Retrieved from https://betterexplained.com/articles/understanding-the-pareto-principle-the-8020-rule/

Buzan, T. (2004, 05/04) In search of genius , BBC Two England . Retrieved from https://www.youtube.com/watch?v=wz_2undwiqY

Calut J-P, (2015). Syllabus Anglais III, Université Saint-Louis, pp. 11-14.

Delengaigne, X. (2011). Apprendre autrement avec les organisateurs graphiques. E-book available on https://www.amazon.fr/kindle/dp/B005N8PNL0/ref=rdr_kindle_ext_eos_detail

Delengaigne, X. (2018, 04/16). J'ai retrouvé les origines du Mind-mapping au Mondanéum. Retrieved from http://www.collectivitenumerique.fr/jai-retrouve-origines-mind-mapping-mundaneum/

Delengaigne, X (2017, 09). Mind-mappeurs: passez au sketch-noting. Rerieved from http://www.collectivitenumerique.fr/tag/sketchnoting/

Franceschi, P. (2003). The dialectic plan: an alternative to the paradigm. *Semiotica* . Vol. 146, pp. 353-367.

Galloway, S. (2017). How Amazon, Google and Facebook manipulate our emotions. Retrieved from: https://www.ted.com/talks/scott_galloway_how_amazon_apple_facebook_and_google_manipulate_our_emotions/transcript#t-761334

Gregory, J. (2004). Writing for the web versus writing for print : Are they really so different ? *Technical Communication,* Vol. 51, Nr. 2.

Keen, R. (2013). The official biography of Tony Buzan: The man who introduced the World to Mind maps. Croydon, UK: Philament Publishing.

Le Bihan, F. , Ambrosini, A., Eichenlaub, V. , de Lardemelle & A. , Pailleau I. (2012). Organisez vos formations avec le Mind-Mapping. Paris: Dunod.

Kleon, A. (2015). How to Make a Newspaper Blackout Poem. Retrieved from https://www.youtube.com/watch?v=wKpVgoGr6kE

Michel (J-F). (2005) Les 7 profils d'apprentissage pour former, enseigner et apprendre. Paris: Eyerolles.

Mueller, P. A. & Oppenheimer, D.M. , (2014). The Pen Is Mightier Than The Keyboard, Advantages of Longhand over Laptop Note Taking. Psychological science. Vol. 25 issue: 6, pp. 1159-1168. doi: 10.1177/0956797614524581

Norman, D. (1993). Things that make us smart : Defending human attributes in the age of the machine. New York: Diversion Books.

Sharples, M., Adams, A., Ferguson, R., Gaved, M., McAndrew, P., Rienties, B., Weller,

M., & Whitelock, D. (2014). *Innovating Pedagogy 2014: Open University Innovation Report 3*. Milton Keynes: The Open University.

Timbal-Duclaux, L. (1983) La méthode SPRI. Organiser ses idées, bien rédiger. Paris: *Retz*.

Wolf, M. and Barzillai, M. (March 2009). The importance of Deep Reading, Educational Leadership, Volume 66, Number 6, Pages 32-37.

Where gadgets go to die (2014, September 14.) *The Economist*. Retrieved from https://www.economist.com/technology-quarterly/2014/09/04/where-gadgets-go-to-die

Webography

NOM	**ADRESSE WEB**	**INFORMATIONS**
Biggerplate	http://www.biggerplate.com/	Biggerplate is the biggest library of mind maps.
Custom writing	https://custom-writing.org/blog/note-taking	40 templates to take notes
Concise learning	http://www.conciselearning.com/	Inspire And Help Students Learn And Be Successful.

Biographies

Madeleine PHILIPPE

Madeleine PHILIPPE is a teacher / trainer in languages (English and French), visual thinking and presentation skills. She has taught and teaches in-company, in adult education and in the academic context. Learning how to learn, Visual thinking and Technologies are at the heart of her approach. She has developed the concept maptelling: Mapping ideas and being able to communicate them (in a foreign language).

Xavier DELENGAIGNE

Xavier DELENGAIGNE is a trainer and consultant in Personal Knowledge Management. His leitmotiv: organize your mind. He's an expert in mind mapping, a graphic method to organize your ideas. He has written 16 books, among which, Learning at high speed, i.e. : Apprendre à toute vitesse published by DUNOD a well-established French publisher.

Franco MASUCCI

Franco MASUCCI is a trainer and consultant on Visual Management. His area of expertise are digital mapping tools. Creator of the ManagementVisuel.fr blog, the use of software to make ideas and projects visual are part of his daily life.

Printed in Great Britain
by Amazon

29327690R00043